Like All Light

Like All Light

Poems

Todd Copeland

Gunpowder Press • Santa Barbara
2022

© 2022 Todd Copeland

Published by Gunpowder Press
David Starkey, Editor
PO Box 60035
Santa Barbara, CA 93160-0035

Cover image: Detail of "Newport Rocks" by John Frederick Kensett, 1872.

ISBN-13: 978-0-9986458-9-6

www.gunpowderpress.com

For my parents

Acknowledgements

I am grateful to the editors of the following publications, in which these poems, sometimes in different forms, first appeared.

Anglican Theological Review: "Hibernal"
Big Sky Journal: "The Rest Is Smoke"
Cagibi: "Song Without Words"
California Quarterly: "Measure Twice, Cut Once"
Columbia Poetry Review: "My Father in the Tree"
Communiqué: "Vernal Equinox"
Christianity and Literature: "Self-Study with Assorted Shadows"
Descant: "Crabbing" and "Nocturne"
Flint Hills Review: "I and I"
Ghost City Review: "Something Triumphal and Everlasting"
High Plains Literary Review: "Middle Bosque Reverie"
I-70 Review: "Limes"
Mudlark: "Special Effects," "Still Life," and "What He Sought in the Forms He Created Was an Irresistible and Inexhaustible Joy"
Pembroke Magazine: "Disjecta Membra"
Potomac Review: "Before Photo"
Relief: A Journal of Art and Faith: "Glimpsed"
River Heron Review: "Last Light at Echo Crater"
Rock & Sling: "Assembling the World in Mid-September"
Sewanee Theological Review: "Moonrise Easter Service"
Southern Poetry Review: "Susan Taking Samples" and "The Tree That Owns Itself"
Spoon River Poetry Review: "Wonders of the World"
Streetlight: "Infra Dig"
Sugar House Review: "The Title of the Poem"
The Adirondack Review: "Twilight"

The Antigonish Review: "Report from November"
The Briar Cliff Review: "Susan at Glistening Waters"
The Cresset: "Golgotha"
The Dalhousie Review: "Moab"
The Journal: "Beachcombing, Matagorda Island," "In Medias Res," "Coastal," and "The Cast Line"
The Other Journal: "Craftsman"
The Texas Observer: "Perihelion" and "Presences"
Valparaiso Poetry Review: "Nine Mile Mountain"

The following poems first appeared in *The Book as Knife*, a chapbook published by Ravenna Press: "Jefferson River Road," "Entre Nous," "Rope-a-Dope," "Just Like Charlie Brown," "The Anatomist's Sketches," "Lacunae," "Amateur Hour," and "The Book as Knife."

Contents

Middle Bosque Reverie	13
Assembling the World in Mid-September	15
Moonrise Easter Service	17
Song Without Words	19
Idyll	20
Seven Sisters	21
My Father in the Tree	22
The Tree That Owns Itself	24
Jefferson River Road	25
Entre Nous	26
The Title of the Poem	27
Rope-a-Dope	28
Beyond Recognition	29
Something Triumphal and Everlasting	30
Making	31
Crabbing	32
War and Peace	34
Prayer to the Thin Line Between Love and Hate	35
The Rest Is Smoke	36
In Medias Res	37
Report from November	39
Susan Taking Samples	40
Susan at Glistening Waters	42
Before Photo	43
Infra Dig	44
Prayer to Loneliness	45
Coastal	46
Wonders of the World	47
Nine Mile Mountain	49
Perihelion	50

Beachcombing, Matagorda Island	51
Prayer to *Blade Runner*'s "Like Tears in Rain" Monologue	52
Just Like Charlie Brown	53
The Anatomist's Sketches	54
Special Effects	55
Lacunae	56
Glimpsed	57
Golgotha	58
Measure Twice, Cut Once	59
Self-Study with Assorted Shadows	60
Last Light at Echo Crater	61
Hibernal	62
Nocturne	63
Vernal Equinox	64
Amateur Hour	65
I and I	66
Limes	67
The Book as Knife	68
Disjecta Membra	69
Twilight	70
Still Life	71
The Dead	72
Split Mountain, Green River, Utah	73
Presences	74
Prayer to March 28, 2020	76
What He Sought in the Forms He Created Was an Irresistible and Inexhaustible Joy	77
Moab	78
Craftsman	79
The Cast Line	81

Middle Bosque Reverie

in memory of William Glen Copeland

Late July lolls along the shallow river
like Narcissus in a swoon,
extravagant and green—
a broad visage of sunlight on water,
the aroma of honeysuckle
strong in late-afternoon heat.

Deep in the bluff's shade,
thick slabs of the Cretaceous riverbed
lie in a group like fallen monuments
to a younger sun; the umbones
of a thousand *Ilymatogyra*
coil out from the ancient bedding plane.

Such a wealth of lost life held fossilized
makes the land's clutch seem permanent.
But it's the decline of place
I notice most—water-worked riverbanks,
scree beneath the limestone bluff.
I find a place to rest and close my eyes.

Of course nothing lasts forever.
Why shouldn't this sun and river
describe time's way? I let the minutes pass
and drowse until my father's father

appears beside me without a word—
his hand extended as a living thing.

I rise in his grasp, and we walk downstream
through an age of water and light and stone
until we reach a bend where the river
widens into a deep pool.

We stop and stand in shared silence
with our backs to the sun, statuesque—
my likeness cast across the water
and only an elegiac brightness
where his shadow should be found.

Assembling the World in Mid-September

Either the harvested cornfield
is a blur of late-summer hues
or it appears itemized and edgy

in stark black-and-white.
The crop remains evident,
cobs and husks mixed with turned earth,

the styles and stigmas of its blond silk
spread across the tract of land—
these things like thrum left on the loom.

Beyond the field and the abandoned
farmhouse, a harrow rusts.
A honey mesquite has grown to maturity

through the middle of its levers and gears,
dropping long pods into the surrounding grass.
The machine is not so much a machine

as it is a memorial to what was.
The mesquite seems poised to lift it,
simulacrum of predator and prey.

A patch of black-and-white fur
blends into dead grass
where I crouch to twist off

a prickly pear's red fruit.
Digging through the hair, I uncover
one small bone, thin as a twig,

and pick it up to hold my future
in my hand. All ampersand,
only the bone connects either with or.

Moonrise Easter Service

At twilight the variations on green
that rimmed the field's expanse
faded to a bluish monochrome, and now,
a quarter to twelve, Easter's constellations
mark the sky—each star gleaming
like a freshly hammered nailhead
tapped flush into the wall of darkness.

Tonight everything seems held in place,
fixed forever as is, while I walk the woods' edge.
Details pass through my flashlight's
small circumference—cow chips, matted grass,
bluebonnets—until, steadying the light,
I pause above the curve of a cow's rib
picked clean and bleached into anonymity.

Nothing can be created out of nothing,
Lucretius said. Things are created
and occasioned without the aid of the gods.
Created out of the darkness of a nearby tree,
an owl skims the rise of the field
at a hard angle away from where I lean on the grass
with the rush of its wings still in my ears.

I pick up the flashlight where it fell by the bone
and aim it out at the night again.
Approaching the field's other edge,
the owl arcs upward and hangs, for a moment,

profiled against a low, rising moon
that's five days from full
and ruddy in the horizon's atmosphere.

We set the little we know of ourselves
against a world of which we know even less.

Song Without Words

for Nancy H. Copeland

The hedge below the kitchen window
softly buzzed with a mid-June music
he and his brother would capture

in plastic bread bags kept on hand.
When the numbers looked right,
they would present the morning's bees

to their mother for a moment of praise.
That embodied music possessed
something of her way with words—

onomatopoetic and consonant-rich,
ready to press back against the world.
The brothers always allowed

the bees to live, returning them
to their fastness of white flowers,
studying how they took to freedom.

In his memory, the morning light
was extravagantly clear as the bees
drifted by the dozens across the hedge

like a run of whole notes in a slow,
wandering melody—the music of an hour
he knew would never be played again.

Idyll

We sometimes rode our bikes to church,
hugging the curb single file,
my athletic father in front, as the road curved

through the only neighborhood I'd known.
His, a lime-green Schwinn,
featured nine more speeds than mine.

My Huffy was black. My handsome father
was a man of sudden enthusiasms.
Sometimes I listened to what he said amid birdsong

and the sounds of passing cars. Mostly not.
Following wandering thoughts
as we biked past my elementary school

straight down Bishop Drive,
I looked for the steeple to come in sight.
Was it possible my young father

suffered a sadness in which he knew
I would one day be clothed?
Our feet traveled in circles. The sun shone.

Seven Sisters

Inside the gloomy lemon-house,
above Lake Garda's blue waters
on a winter morning, the ruddy oranges
clustered low along a path
reminded Lawrence of village lights
along the shore at night,
while the pale lemons, hanging above
in ghostly trees, resembled stars.

The fragrant fruit of words
written more than a century ago
bring to mind the time my father
showed me the Seven Sisters
when I was a boy, his finger aimed
toward a region of the heavens
where, gradually, I discerned,
clustered together and faintly
glowing, a small haze of stars.

Wary of being tricked,
I counted as each of the Pleiades
intermittently emerged while we sat
side by side in the front yard
of our home on Westlawn Drive—
separate worlds and yet
bound up together in distant stars.

My Father in the Tree

The pecan tree looming over the yard
seemed to govern the sky
with its green crown.

My father was lost in his work
between its branches, putting a torch
to the caterpillars' gauzy gray webs

that hung like caught clouds
among the leaves. Six years old,
I stretched out in the shade

and studied the familiar figure
moving overhead. My father the dentist,
with his rod of fire, was healing

the infested tree. The slaughter was certain.
Shriveling webs described
each slow sweep of flame

as dark spots of larvae disappeared,
a faint play of smoke
their final attribute. Hellish hands.

I couldn't read my father's face
behind the light-blue mask from work,
but his eyes had that look

of inscrutable concentration
I'd seen before, in his chair,
as he worked on my mouth.

I bore silent witness
to a slowly transpiring change:
The longer he labored from limb to limb,

taking life left and right,
the less he appeared to merely inhabit
that kingdom of leaves

and the more his ownership
seemed absolute. My father took
his time, lord of the tree and more.

I was left wondering how soon,
and to what end, he would carry
that fire toward earth and me.

The Tree That Owns Itself

Athens, Georgia

Most noble boozers,
and you my very esteemed and poxy friends,
he said, cribbing Rabelais.

He was at The Globe
but would soon be lured outdoors
in the dead of Appalachian winter
to behold the legendary tree
that stood a half mile from downtown.

What did it know of freedom,
this tree that never knew it had been owned,
he asked the others,
this tree so pampered
even the public road curved around it?
He feigned melodrama,
sprawling out beneath its wide branches
and pretending himself buried
in a solitary grave.

O to be dead and gone
and done with life, he would say.
He had no pride.
He didn't even know what kind of tree it was.

Jefferson River Road

Sure, we saw him plenty around town,
going into Wuxtry,
browsing the aisles at Jackson Street Books,
always in those cotton dress shirts
bought at Goodwill.

It was 1991, the year punk broke,
but we knew nothing
would ever feel as good
as dancing to side A of *Doolittle*
with that other Todd.

No one suspected the chaos of his heart,
the extremity of his desire.
He was doomed from the start,
we said, for all his careful artistry.

O sweet, feigned innocence.
O newlywed Dionysus
in a small house among the pines.

Entre Nous

We had long sought escape
among the multicolored lights
of the inked city,
in the understory of the unpaginated woods.

But it wasn't meant to be,
no matter how often
we read Proust late into the night.
My bon ami, we were never much of a talker,
even when those mornings
in Marseille turned balmy.

We were a rather simple machine
putting together strings of words.
We were always just ourselves.

The Title of the Poem

A century or so later,
we sensed the era of freedom had passed.
Our art had become a thing of suggestion,
the product of contingency,
the child of a father
whose path demanded following.

We were free to think we had choices.
Our colors were pale blue and citrus yellow.

Rope-a-Dope

We could feel someone
thumbing through our pages.
Our life as a book was a slim thing
though we came unabridged.

They thought they could get the better of us,
kick us to the curb once they were done.
They presumed words were *words*.

But our typeface, sans serif,
was meant to beguile,
to lure them in so close our world
would encompass them and never die.

Beyond Recognition

They claimed
the fountain was inconsequential,
but we knew better.

Blue springs flowed without ceasing.

Headquarters said look around,
everything is based on a true story.
The verisimilitude is sufficient.

Seriously? We acted blasé.
Blah, blah, blah, blah, blah.
A little voice said aspire to the source,
screw cinéma vérité
and all other agents of artifice.

What abides remains unseen.

Something Triumphal and Everlasting

Like the sweeping melody
of "Hark! the Herald Angels Sing"
but times eleventy million.

Or like when we saw Nirvana
play the 40 Watt
in that transfiguring fall of 1991.

Remember?
After ending their set with "Aneurysm,"
totally hammered,
they destroyed their gear
amid a chaos of distortion
that felt, in the moment,
never-ending and inescapable.

Making

The stoneware jug, ovoid
and decorated with an incised anchor
and two American flags,

sits in the Smithsonian
bearing his maker's mark:
"W. Lundy & Co., Troy," circa 1826.

My Irish ancestor
William Lundy studies these words
taking shape left to right.

We are joined in hands-on work,
the potter and I, the side of my palm
pressed to the page—a steady base

for the pen's sure strokes.
I handle each word
with a craftsman's care,

his touch alive in mine.
Let us, then, make something
that never existed before.

Crabbing

Blue crabs dangled like acrobats
from noosed chicken necks,
their red-tipped claws clamped tight
as the creatures slowly ascended
toward my brother and me.

We hauled up our lines hand over fist
from Copano Bay's shallow,
moonlit waters. Rockport, Texas,
circa any childhood summer.

We would stand among the men
fishing beneath big, humming lights
that created oases of flying insects
down the old causeway's length.
Our father always chatted up anyone
standing nearby, sharing stories
that took embellished turns.

He had taught us how to grab crabs
from behind, their waving claws
as ineffective as our protests
against getting the belt.
There was that side to him
we tried to avoid, the unnerving smile
anger forced across his face.

My brother and I tossed our catch
into a plastic bucket with casualness.

The crabs clattered and climbed
one another with bubbling mouths—
captives to be boiled alive,
turned into red devils,
and ripped apart, limb by limb.

War and Peace

Birds were more interesting dead
than alive. From my father
I learned the art of finding
what fell, fluttering, from the sky.

Brought to earth, held in my small hands,
doves became the playthings
of my unlettered imagination.
I esteemed their crimson eyes and fanned feathers;
their bodies weighed next to nothing
tucked against the small of my back.

Mallards were another fascination,
green-headed drakes lined up
near a lake's edge outside El Campo.

I would help deploy the decoys
then wait beside my father in the blind.
When the ducks came wheeling across
the early-morning sky, they were like
the comet above Prechistensky Boulevard
that answered to the new life blossoming
in Pierre's soul. Soon, I knew,
I would hold fast their flight.

Prayer to the Thin Line Between Love and Hate

Not the Pretenders song,
although Chrissie Hynde's vibrato
and dark bangs hanging
over her eyebrows just so
surely merit supplication.

And not even the original
by The Persuaders,
despite all its charms.

No, this prayer is lifted up
to the actual thin line
between love and hate.

You know the one—
that moment wearing its thinness
like an advertisement,
proud of how easy it is
for the heart to break one way
or the other across its razor's edge.

The Rest Is Smoke

His brother grew smaller
and smaller as the train
pulled away. Finally,
there was nothing left.

Decades later,
he remembered the scene
while standing in the modest
darkness of a summer dusk

on a hillside north of
Deer Lodge, Montana,
silent like his nearby friends,
as they listened to,

and even slightly felt,
nighthawks diving and
swooping past
like half-glimpsed truths.

In Medias Res

Like signals, Port O'Connor's pier lights
blink off and on behind us
as we troll toward the open water
of the Gulf of Mexico.

The coast slowly shapes itself
out of the dark as the pre-dawn sky
turns dark blue and then brightens
into ultramarine, erasing last night's stars.

Half an hour later, I steer the boat
through a cut in the barrier island
where, ahead and to the left,
the sun inches upward from sky and water's seam
and becomes entire. My father's friend,
finishing another beer, raises a hand
toward the low, bull's-eye sun.
Extending index finger and thumb,
he frames the fire and pretend-carries it to me.

Meanwhile, the saga of daybreak
has put my father to sleep. His graying head
wobbles on a pillow of life preservers
pushed against the live-bait well.

In the rough waves between the jetty's arms
he wakes and says his favorite fishing joke.
His friend groans. My father laughs twice
and absent-mindedly scratches

his psoriatic arm. I steer. The Gulf's mouth
opens between two gonging buoys.

Looking back over my shoulder,
I watch the Vs of the boat's wake
tail off into the shelving waves where
a dolphin breaches, blows, and disappears.

Dawn has broken for the multi-billionth time.
What are our lives in comparison?

Report from November

for Todd Hearon

I turn to climb the bluff
that runs along the river's wide mirror.
The nuances of November

grow more distinct with height,
the doubled browns and greens of trees.
It's been said that specialization,

leading one to speak more and more
about less and less, will culminate
in everything being said about nothing.

But what about saying less and less
about more and more? On the other bank,
two deer drink from the river.

Their heads quickly rise. They turn
and become a perfect simple sentence,
single verb following single noun.

Susan Taking Samples

Sprawled out beside a bristlecone pine,
you hang head and arms over the mesa's rim
scouring sandstone strata for something

to remove, label, study further, and, ultimately,
shelve. Your hair's one braid dangles
from your nape in a double helix while,

two hundred feet below, the shale slopes gleam
with flakes of mica in the midmorning sunlight.
Miles to the south, the badlands extend

to a hazy horizon. Shouldering an hour's work,
you carry the landscape away into
southwestern Colorado, around hogback and hoodoo,

past butte and cuesta, down a mining shaft
near Telluride where your fingers trace veins
of gold-rich ore deep within one

of a thousand mountains. Alone for a week,
I've succumbed to remembering you
through your rock collection.

I dawdle in the closet-stacked boxes
like a lover cooing pet names—basalt, feldspar,
pumice, quartz. I think of you sleeping

in the Rockies in our wedding-present tent,
shivering yourself awake to find the campsite silver
beneath the moon's gloriole. Nights,

I dream of your face adumbrated in the black glass
of obsidian—metamorphic, surrounded
by the passing beauty of living things.

Susan at Glistening Waters

On my own three weeks this time,
I moon through the evening hours
itemizing the odds and ends of loneliness.

I observe our anniversary
by finding your coordinates
in Rand McNally's Atlas of the World
and re-reading your postcards
from Jamaica until I can almost see
the bay's microscopic life
glowing, at night,
around the contours of your body.

Life's timing is all wrong.
I've taken your pillow for mine,
its fragrance mixed with the scent of mimosa
wafting in through the open window.

Before Photo

Time came as clouds
crossing the sky in silence.
The world had no origin

before today.
A sentence, like a sky,
is a question or an answer,

depending. Sunlight
touches our bodies
with impermanence at noon,

and the trees overhead shine
underneath. What could possibly
astonish us after now?

Infra Dig

You know how when the sky
goes to hell in the west
there's inevitably a black dot of a bird
moving slowly, often left to right,
across its expanse and you admit,
although you know it's something
that shouldn't be said,
considering God granted us dominion,
that, despite being small,
such a bird possibly matters more
to the world than yourself?

Prayer to Loneliness

from a letter by James Wright

"My own attacks—
a strong word,
but an accurate one—

of unhappiness
come in the form
of an awful, perhaps indescribable

loneliness.
It is not a loneliness
of the body—there are plenty

of people around,
in New York, especially—
but a loneliness of the soul,

in which I feel
an appalling sense
of abandonment and loss."

Coastal

A Norwegian tanker crosses
Corpus Christi Bay toward the tall arch
of the channel-spanning bridge
and the row of refineries just beyond.
A minute later, everything is as it was before—
horizon uninterrupted, late-afternoon sun,
each wave graced
with the sunlight of early November.

Is there a pattern, pointless or not,
to the hours slipping away,
to our brief lives sailing out in small craft
across the sun-struck water?

Something in our blood makes us
stare out to sea with thoughts of being
someone else anywhere else
than in this coastal city, Christ's nominal body,
where chronic fishermen gamble the cost of bait
along the business district's sea wall
and each oil refinery's thousand lights illuminate
midnight darkness like a dense mass of false stars.

Along the reach of a nearby pier, one to a post,
a dozen gulls stare like magi into the breeze.
A crab's carapace bobs in the dark water.
What music, if any, drifts across the waves?

Wonders of the World

We had taken the elevator deep underground,
five souls from the surface,
and been led through the Hall of Giants.

You would never have known it was January,
much less New Mexico, above.
The place felt nowhere, outside time.

Back-lit draperies.
Columns thicker than the Parthenon's.

My sons were young then—
a perfect span of ages for the stories
my father was waiting to share
at his ranch near Mayhill.

Who knows what they thought of it all?

They did as told when the park ranger
performed her set piece
like Charon must have done,
untold times, before shoving off—
each boy's palm an inch from his face
when she killed the lights
and sent us into a darkness absolute.

How long would it last,
everything unknowable by sight?
I remember looking

for my sons' faces and finding nothing.
And then, in three days' time,
my father was gone from this world,
like a myth. Like all light.

Nine Mile Mountain

I leave snowshoe tracks
in a winter's worth of powder
that my son follows for a time

before making his own way
up the mountain. At ten,
alive in this snow-filled Arcadia,

why wouldn't he believe his steps
could be his alone? That our tracks
left behind in the quiet forest

will soon guide our return?
When my father died near Cloudcroft,
the ambulance speeding down

toward the Tularosa Basin,
I followed fifteen minutes behind.
He was always in the lead.

In the hospital, near the body,
his black work boots stood alone
on a countertop as if waiting

for use by the back door at home.
My father will never rest in peace.
I imagine his figure up ahead

moving among the ascendant pines,
his snowy steps waiting for ours
to come to life, to shape oblivion.

Perihelion

What could be more easily neglected
than the day after New Year's Day,
an anticlimax's anticlimax?
The date's sole distinction is its lack of status,
a vagabond staring down a long road
that narrows to a point in the blue distance.

Along a stretch of land overlooking the river,
fallen leaves hem the posts of a barbed-wire fence,
as plentiful as already abandoned resolutions.
Another orbit over, the holidays having come
and gone again, this second day of January
seems the *sine qua non* of nothing special.

Yet I prefer the overlooked to the overt.
I tend toward the penultimate,
the peripheral or indistinct, and so,
today, the sun defines a thousand things,
the bare trees throwing figures across the river
that inform what they touch like prophecy.

Beachcombing, Matagorda Island

The wind felt cold and terminal.
Rain began falling on the remote beach.
Late afternoon, late November.
Everything was out of season
except the ends of things.

Sand dollars, unloaded on a table,
overlapped one another like actual
and imagined lives. Taking one in hand,
he touched thumbs across the test's
slight swell and broke it open
down the diameter of its circumscribed,
five-armed star. A few taps delivered
the Aristotle's lantern's five white jaws
into the creases of his palm.
He studied the small, winged things.

Mellita quinquiesperforata.
Taxonomy seemed a weak stay
against namelessness. To his right,
the barrier island's dunes receded
in mimicry of waves. To his left,
the coastal waters darkened
like Nebuchadnezzar's dreams.

Prayer to *Blade Runner*'s "Like Tears in Rain" Monologue

You fall decorously
from Batty's lips
with the slightest of British accents
and an almost human pathos
into Deckard's ears.

Each moment of your words
expires amid
blue shadows and rain.

Your creator could have let
his adversary fall to death,
not saved him in the grip
of a nail-pierced hand,
but an audience was required
to give meaning to those C-beams
glittering in the dark
near the Tannhäuser Gate.

"Time to die."
But you are deathless.
Spoken. Heard.

Just Like Charlie Brown

We knew things about him.
That, as a child,
he rocked himself to sleep every night.
That his pleasant demeanor
hid brokenness.
We even knew he liked to imagine himself
as Jean-Michel Basquiat on occasion.

His vulnerabilities seemed sweet,
endearing even,
but then *they* told us
we looked like a house of cards,
said we'd become their bête noire.

We had lived our life thinking
it was third and manageable.
Try fourth and forever, they said.

The Anatomist's Sketches

Late one night, slightly drunk,
he remembered being hammered
at stupid o'clock atop a boxcar,
rolling past the old General Tire plant
and Bellmead's empty streets,
where traffic lights changed for no one.

We sought to make of him our home,
to stop despising people
who wished us a happy day,
to have him become as liminal to our existence
as the thick lines
defining Matisse's languorous nudes.

Was movement as solution the solution?
He seemed to suggest so.
He recollected traveling on a train
south of St. Louis, deep into the night,
where a bargeman's searchlight
swept across the moon-reflecting Mississippi.

Special Effects

Wasn't it enough that we showed up
almost on time each day?
We straightened his striped tie
and sent him out ahead of us
to be sociable. We made an effort,
sometimes, to do something
resembling honest work,
but more than our heart just not
being in it our mind was miles away
in la-la land, out in space where we
zipped past Jupiter's Galilean moons,
rapidly approaching the speed of light.

Lacunae

We were like those spaces at Pompeii,
gaps in ash detailing the shapes
bodies made as they crouched
in corners of houses or fell, terrorized,
to grooved cobblestones.

He was busy with questions,
his wet skin glowing in the late-afternoon light
of early autumn.
We said we hate to be a person
on business from Porlock,
but you should be aware the dead control us
through the mortmain of song.

We were like a cicada's nymphal husk
clinging to pine bark
in an attitude of inescapable prayer,
as emptied as Christ in Gethsemane.

He insisted the body had a hidden life.
No, we said. There's only emptiness.

Glimpsed

Saint Cuthbert
left the monastery of Lindisfarne
for the kind of blessed solitude we craved,
the blues and whites of his Northumbrian noon
a balm to both mind and soul.

We preferred
picturing him in his last hours,
his bed pulled to a window
in the island hermitage where,
between blocks of roughhewn stone,
cormorants would flash
across an allowance of sky.

The deep shadows of dusk
would have slowly filled his room,
pagan and nonspecific,
the coming night a final darkness
through which waving torches
would signal his life's end
across water to Holy Island.

Golgotha

for Karl Umlauf

The frame defines the anthology of skulls
examined from above as if through
the open hatch of a cellar come to by chance.

We kneel, lean over, and look in,
all of our lives to lose or gain.
Chiaroscurist of the afterworld,

the place of skulls is limitless.
But we see only what you've
brought to light, made plain,

and signed in the bottom left-hand corner
with prescience—the hoard of death's-heads
streaked ocher and rust

unearthed from a common grave.
Below or above isn't the issue.
The depths overhead yield equally.

Take a boy in a park on a spring day
watching his kite's skeletal cross
travel the blue sky. He lets the kite climb,

the string connecting him to it
unwinding off the humming spool
into the long sag, excavating light.

Measure Twice, Cut Once

White walls held Rothko's Rothkos.
Like windows or mirrors,
the canvases invited sight.

One saw through or in them—
among fields of blue and green,
yellow and white—an exactness of life.

Self-Study with Assorted Shadows

I follow my long shadow,
running down a stretch of rural road
in a marathoner's trance
under July's indiscriminate sun.

Lux est umbra Dei—
perhaps it's true.

My shadow, then, twice-removed
from pure illumination.
I cast myself as Everyman,
companionless and peregrine,
a runner for years and still
nowhere near anything of note
though I catalogue my steps
as if they were aimed toward
some ultima Thule of our age.

Trading in solitudes and silences,
a taste of salt in my dry mouth,
why hope to find beatitude
chasing after my body's dark star?

Flushed from a windbreak,
birds sweep low over a field of sorghum
ready for harvest—black doors
to the bronze intricacies of summer.

Last Light at Echo Crater

for Gary Chipman

The leitmotif of the land's rise and fall
forms our horizon. Ancient lava flows
run for miles beyond the great rift
and the caldera's rim—black,
inhospitable acres of pahoehoe and aa—
while the surrounding terrain
offers a still life in sage and cinder
to the foot of the worn mountains
cast in the bluish twilight of central Idaho.

Our midsummer tour through the West.
Tell me, what does it mean to be old friends?

In the dusk, away from it all,
we take turns yelling obscenities
at our small camp hundreds of feet below,
and the depths of the cinder cone's crater
reciprocate our words—answer back,
at intervals, with the timbre of stone.

Strange to hear profanity made so disembodied—
such a recessive, dull refrain. Stranger still
to find us here, silenced side by side,
taking in the view of someplace between somewhere
and somewhere else where neither of us belongs.
What were our expectations? Should we
have hoped to find more than who we aren't?

Hibernal

Late February, the darkness
ecumenical beneath the night's new moon.

Another norther filigrees
fallen leaves and windowpanes
with a delicate, light frost.
Why draw a line between
the living and the dead
on such a night, when the darkness
within everything everywhere
acknowledges itself?

One stares through a window
at the allusive, bituminous view,
a ghost of breath upon the glass,
once again the unborn child who,
after six months in the womb,
opens his eyes for the first time
and finds the comprehensive darkness
the mother holds within herself.

Nocturne

The mother sings to the three boys—
ages six, four, and two—
who lie on their backs in the middle
of their beds and stare
into dark corners. The children's eyes
close and open and close.

By the second lullaby's closing refrain,
all three are asleep.
But their mother sings a third song
and then remains where
she's been kneeling, slightly moonlit,
in the middle of the room.

Vernal Equinox

The purity of what remains
at one remove always came to mind
during long, penitential dusks,

when his heart, filled with misgivings,
seemed one with the river valley
turning bluish-gray by degrees

and the brawl of tree limbs
losing definition as night drew near.
Looking back in such a mood,

he ritualized his life's regrets
against the darkening stretch of sky.
The purity of what remains

at one remove is a religion of desire,
a soft light set against the known
on certain nights. He watched

the final traces of dusk fade
as stars grew bright in the sky
like a tableau vivant of the absolutes.

Amateur Hour

We observed we were American by way,
in reverse order,
of Quebec, Jamaica, and Ulster.

Why bother being explainable?

We fancied the idea of there being
a specific type of nothing
for each kind of something.
Infinitude possessed a perfectly
understandable appeal, but one
grew tired in its contemplation.

We bid the world's demands adieu,
retired to our chambers for the night,
vowed to sleep until whenever.

I and I

The last time we heard from him
he said he'd just realized
his driveway was connected
to every road in North America.

He spoke of an expanse of darkness
and the fear that everything he did
was for the last time.

We had no answers.
Our body hungered only for dreams
day and night.

Limes

He told us it felt like standing
on the heights of Mycenae above the Argolid
and its expanse of orange orchards and olive trees.

Not that he imagined himself an Agamemnon.
It was more the sense, having hazarded greatness,
of being lost in time, he said.

We wondered if he realized
how ridiculous he sounded,
spiffed and doing his philosophy bit.

We knew escaping into the sky
was too obvious a solution,
so we went inside ourselves like a flood of solitude.
Daily life came to feel as if
it had been lived in for centuries,
like a church.

After so very many years
in this world, he said,
the taste of the great poem of life
is less like limes
and more that of a caraway seed—
a crescent-shaped bitterness
that slowly sweetens the mouth.

The Book as Knife

While our continent
became a charnel house,
other lands remained a consoling mystery.

What were the green words
children said in play over there?

Water always takes
the easiest path available,
bloody or not.

Our poems were small disasters,
our book a knife of little use.

Disjecta Membra

We washed ashore
after calamities beyond numbering.
The misshapen dead lay about us,
unlettered, like forgetfulness.

Figures took shape in the sand
behind our fingertips.
We prayed to the Ancient of Days.
We fed on shadows.

People lived in us.
Our pain sang
like so many scattered beads in the sun.

Twilight

We traveled north down the Nile to Abydos,
the boat's oarsmen slaves to a rhythm.
They said we were dead.
Osiris was waiting.

It was the first we'd heard about it.
We wanted to know
was life retrievable, we wanted to return.
Could this trip be deleted like email or a text?

We pictured the clouds massing
above the Pacific near Tofino,
how the light looked at the end of the day
on the last day of July years ago.
A cloud's requirement of sky.
The light's last act.

We argued that the song of a god
previously unknown to man
was calling us back to the moment
just after there was no time.

There a trapezoid of light
traveled across clean hardwood floors.

Still Life

Distant mountains called to us.
So distant they couldn't be seen.
So mountainous as to be monolithic.

The distance between here and there
seemed incalculable.

A call so loud it verged on noise.
An us so *us* we got confused
and wondered aloud if we were rock.

We looked for him everywhere
to gain his perspective but learned
he'd given up being a people-pleaser
and had gone solo to Sri Lanka for the month.
They said his face was inscrutable,
his brows like diacritical marks
above the blue vowels of his eyes.

The mountains were not green.
We were not feeling ourselves.
The calling was incessant,
driving us to cover our ears.

Like it or not, they said,
you have to live in this world—
in person and for one time only.

The Dead

We grant the dead
strange life
in our dreams.

They stand before us,
unaged, like nothing
happened. We want
to know what
they mean, their music,
how they look inside.

Their lives
are over
before they know it.

Split Mountain, Green River, Utah

Swallow nests' round
mouths chorus up
the nearby cliff face

while beyond
the swirling current
massive sandstone strata
tilt both skyward
and into the earth.

What right could I
possibly have
to live forever,
or even just this once?

Presences

Any month would do. Any day, in fact.
But let's imagine some midmorning

in early June as the neighborhood's trees
gather an abundance of light

and a mourning dove coos somewhere unseen
when we, in a moment of abstraction,

forget ourselves among the many pleasures
and extent of life. There's always

the possibility of never coming back,
an idea the Jains of ancient India

crafted into a shrine I once saw on display.
The small metal box, open on one side,

revealed a person's simplified figure
rendered, at the back, in reverse silhouette—

a shape of light cut into the dark square.
The miniature body, a placard explained,

was the paradoxical absence of itself.
A portrait of achieved release.

To the eye, however, the body was whatever
lay behind the shrine—a shape of grass,

perhaps, or, in a museum, polished stone.
Just as John Cage's *4'33"* was not,

as its first puzzled audience assumed,
a performance of silence but a composition,

in three parts, of the rediscovered world
a piano's bright silence contains.

Prayer to March 28, 2020

Your hours are like a well
to be filled with tossed pennies,
as James Tate might say.

Your morning light
like a lesson
in loving without hesitation.

Your words like those
Aeneas spoke to his father,
carrying him from roaring flames:
"Whatever falls to us now,
we both will share one peril."

Your clouds of early spring
are like the ways of men
are like the hounds of love are like
nights spent as alone as the last man
on the face of the earth or like
the days of our youth
that are not unlike, if one
considers the matter with
helplessness, a summer of clouds.

What He Sought in the Forms He Created
Was an Irresistible and Inexhaustible Joy

He was drawn to the decorum
of short lines in trim stanzas.

Sometimes what the words meant
mattered less than the eye's journey
through quatrains linked
like the small towns along Highway 6
going northwest from town:
Valley Mills, Clifton,
Meridian, Hico, Dublin.

He shared the ancient Greeks' cast of mind,
drawn to an exactitude of form
irresistible in its perfection.

He dreamed of his poems
setting sail like an argosy.

Moab

"All arches are but temporary features
and all will eventually succumb
to the forces of gravity and erosion,"

a sign near the Devil's Garden read.
People of many nations crossed
the reddish-orange Utah landscape

toward Delicate Arch. A month since
calling it quits, finally, he had met middle age
beneath a catastrophe of desert light.

Why try to spell it all out?
His thoughts wouldn't line up right.
Down on Center Street, below

the canyon's sheer sandstone walls,
he took in the pale blue sky and recited
"The Planet on the Table." That night,

in the cooling breeze, he stepped out
into the glissando of alien tongues and,
as resolutely as Ruth, entered foreign land.

Craftsman

After fixing people's teeth all day,
my father remained at his office,
alone amid dental impressions

and plaster models, etching my initials
into Sears Craftsman tools.
His painstaking labor embraced

even the slenderest of things—
"WTC" gleaming silvery
against the matte black of a short-arm,

two-millimeter Allen key.
Each ratchet and socket bore my name.
Every screwdriver.

Every wrench.
Conspicuously heavy, inexpertly wrapped,
the stainless steel toolbox

anchored our Christmas tree
when I was thirteen. Today, like a gift,
news of the Sears bankruptcy

brings all this back. Now fifty,
and sentimental, I lift the dinged-up lid
to inventory what remains

of my father's handiwork among
the hodgepodge of intervening years.
If you loan someone your tools,

he told me, forget ever seeing them again.
Volunteer to help instead.
Some days I forget I'll never

see my father again. Gone into death,
he lingers, for a time,
in the graven lines of my name.

The Cast Line

in memory of William Chad Copeland

The water has the shine of worked gold
where the low sun replicates itself,
refulgent and oblong, across Aransas Bay.

Forty yards offshore, working a wharf's
barnacled pilings for redfish and trout,
my father and I stand sideways to the glare—

human from the waist up, ocean below.
There's an eroticism to these early hours,
the spuming combers exhausting themselves

in an aubade on the landward slope,
the matutinal wind soft on the back of the neck.
Morning brings back the heroic ages,

Thoreau said, and perhaps he's right.
Beyond Rockport's bait shops
and greasy spoons, past houses on stilts

down the dirt road out of town
where wild grass and oleander border
the shoreline's thin strip of crushed shells,

my father's touched by an air of the fabulous
that suggests it's not so much real life
he lives but some charmed perfection of it.

Slowly, his arm goes back. The rod
ranges the sky. The slender shadow
of his cast line lives on the bright water.

About the Poet

Todd Copeland's *Like All Light* was selected by Lynne Thompson for the 2021 Barry Spacks Poetry Prize. His other works include the poetry chapbook *The Book as Knife* (Ravenna Press, 2021) and the narrative nonfiction book *The Immortal Ten* (Baylor University Press, 2006). His poems have appeared in *The Journal, Southern Poetry Review, Valparaiso Poetry Review, Lake Effect, Christianity & Literature,* and *Sugar House Review,* among other publications, and his essays have been published in such journals as *Literary Imagination, JNT: Journal of Narrative Theory,* and *Media, War & Conflict*. He holds degrees in English from Baylor University (BA), The University of Georgia (MA), and Texas A&M University (PhD). A native of Ohio, he lives in Waco, Texas.

BARRY SPACKS POETRY PRIZE SERIES

2015
Instead of Sadness
Catherine Abbey Hodges

2016
Burning Down Disneyland
Kurt Olsson

2017
Posthumous Noon
Aaron Baker

2018
The Ghosts of Lost Animals
Michelle Bonczek Evory

2019
Drinking with O'Hara
Glenn Freeman

2020
Curriculum
Meghan Dunn

2021
Like All Light
Todd Copeland

Also from Gunpowder Press

The Tarnation of Faust: Poems by David Case

Mouth & Fruit: Poems by Chryss Yost

Shaping Water: Poems by Barry Spacks

Original Face: Poems by Jim Peterson

What Breathes Us: Santa Barbara Poets Laureate, 2005-2015
Edited by David Starkey

Unfinished City: Poems by Nan Cohen

Raft of Days: Poems by Catherine Abbey Hodges

Mother Lode: Poems by Peg Quinn

and the Shoreline Voices Projects:

Buzz: Poets Respond to SWARM
Edited by Nancy Gifford and Chryss Yost

Rare Feathers: Poems on Birds & Art
Edited by Nancy Gifford, Chryss Yost, and George Yatchisin

To Give Life a Shape: Poems Inspired by the Santa Barbara Museum of Art
Edited by David Starkey and Chryss Yost

While You Wait: A Collection by Santa Barbara County Poets
Edited by Laure-Anne Bosselaar

*Big Enough for Words: Poems and Vintage Photographs
from California's Central Coast*
Edited by David Starkey, George Yatchisin, and Chryss Yost